MACBETH

THE FOLIO EDITION

WILLIAM SHAKESPEARE

P9-CJM-395

ILLUSTRATED BY VON

WORKMAN PUBLISHING
NEW YORK

Edited and Produced by Oval Projects Limited, London.
Copyright © 1982 Oval Projects Limited
Illustration copyright © 1982 Von
All rights reserved. No portion of this book may
be reproduced — mechanically, electronically, or
by any other means now known or herein after invented,
without permission of the publisher.
Published simultaneously in Canada by Saunders of Toronto, Inc.

Cover design: Louise Fili

Library of Congress Cataloging in Publication Data
Shakespeare, William, 1564-1616
The illustrated Macbeth.

I. Von.   II. Title.
PR2823.A2V6   1982   822.3'3   81-43787
ISBN 0-89480-205-4   AACR2

Workman Publishing Company, Inc.
1 West 39 Street
New York, New York 10018
Manufactured in Hong Kong
First printing April 1982
10 9 8 7 6 5 4 3 2 1

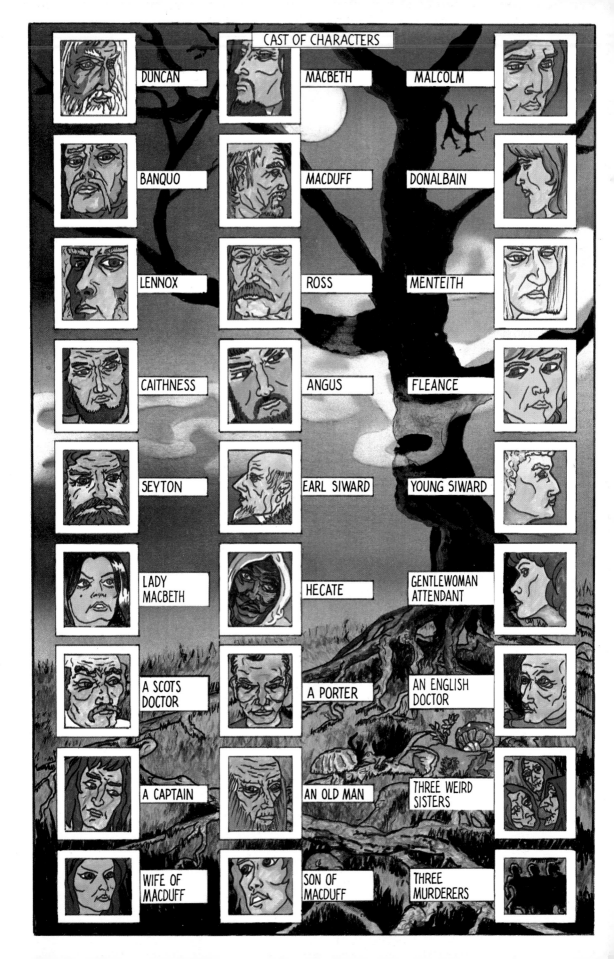

4

5

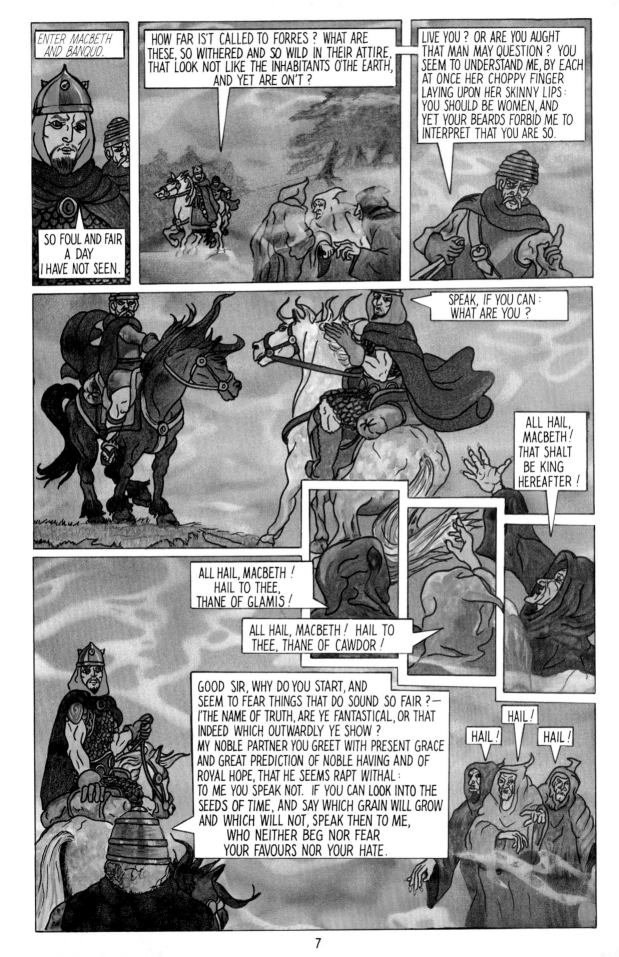

ENTER ROSS AND ANGUS.

WHO'S HERE?

THE KING HATH HAPPILY RECEIVED, MACBETH, THE NEWS OF THY SUCCESS; AND WHEN HE READS THY PERSONAL VENTURE IN THE REBELS' FIGHT, HIS WONDERS AND HIS PRAISES DO CONTEND WHICH SHOULD BE THINE OR HIS. SILENCED WITH THAT, IN VIEWING O'ER THE REST O'THE SELFSAME DAY, HE FINDS THEE IN THE STOUT NORWEYAN RANKS, NOTHING AFEARD OF WHAT THYSELF DIDST MAKE, STRANGE IMAGES OF DEATH. AS THICK AS HAIL CAME POST WITH POST, AND EVERYONE DID BEAR THY PRAISES IN HIS KINGDOM'S GREAT DEFENCE, AND POURED THEM DOWN BEFORE HIM.

WE ARE SENT TO GIVE THEE FROM OUR ROYAL MASTER THANKS; ONLY TO HERALD THEE INTO HIS SIGHT, NOT PAY THEE.

AND, FOR AN EARNEST OF A GREATER HONOUR, HE BADE ME, FROM HIM, CALL THEE THANE OF CAWDOR: IN WHICH ADDITION, HAIL, MOST WORTHY THANE, FOR IT IS THINE.

WHAT! CAN THE DEVIL SPEAK TRUE?

THE THANE OF CAWDOR LIVES: WHY DO YOU DRESS ME IN BORROWED ROBES?

WHO WAS THE THANE LIVES YET; BUT UNDER HEAVY JUDGEMENT BEARS THAT LIFE WHICH HE DESERVES TO LOSE. WHETHER HE WAS COMBINED WITH THOSE OF NORWAY, OR DID LINE THE REBEL WITH HIDDEN HELP AND VANTAGE, OR THAT WITH BOTH HE LABOURED IN HIS COUNTRY'S WRACK, I KNOW NOT; BUT TREASONS CAPITAL, CONFESSED AND PROVED, HAVE OVERTHROWN HIM.

GLAMIS, AND THANE OF CAWDOR! THE GREATEST IS BEHIND.

THANKS FOR YOUR PAINS. — DO YOU NOT HOPE YOUR CHILDREN SHALL BE KINGS, WHEN THOSE THAT GAVE THE THANE OF CAWDOR TO ME PROMISED NO LESS TO THEM?

THAT, TRUSTED HOME, MIGHT YET ENKINDLE YOU UNTO THE CROWN, BESIDES THE THANE OF CAWDOR. BUT 'TIS STRANGE: AND OFTENTIMES, TO WIN US TO OUR HARM, THE INSTRUMENTS OF DARKNESS TELL US TRUTHS, WIN US WITH HONEST TRIFLES, TO BETRAY'S IN DEEPEST CONSEQUENCE. COUSINS, A WORD, I PRAY YOU.

TWO TRUTHS ARE TOLD, AS HAPPY PROLOGUES TO THE SWELLING ACT OF THE IMPERIAL THEME.

16

IF IT WERE DONE WHEN 'TIS DONE, THEN 'TWERE WELL IT WERE DONE QUICKLY. IF THE ASSASSINATION COULD TRAMMEL UP THE CONSEQUENCE, AND CATCH WITH HIS SURCEASE SUCCESS; THAT BUT THIS BLOW MIGHT BE THE BE-ALL AND THE END-ALL. HERE, BUT HERE, UPON THIS BANK AND SHOAL OF TIME, WE'D JUMP THE LIFE TO COME.

BUT IN THESE CASES WE STILL HAVE JUDGEMENT HERE; THAT WE BUT TEACH BLOODY INSTRUCTIONS, WHICH, BEING TAUGHT, RETURN TO PLAGUE THE INVENTOR. THIS EVEN-HANDED JUSTICE COMMENDS THE INGREDIENCE OF OUR POISONED CHALICE TO OUR OWN LIPS. HE'S HERE IN DOUBLE TRUST: FIRST, AS I AM HIS KINSMAN AND HIS SUBJECT, STRONG BOTH AGAINST THE DEED; THEN, AS HIS HOST,

TRUMPET-TONGUED AGAINST THE DEEP DAMNATION OF HIS TAKING-OFF; AND PITY, LIKE A NAKED NEW-BORN BABE, STRIDING THE BLAST, OR HEAVEN'S CHERUBIN, HORSED UPON THE SIGHTLESS COURIERS OF THE AIR, SHALL BLOW THE HORRID DEED IN EVERY EYE, THAT TEARS SHALL DROWN THE WIND.

WHO SHOULD AGAINST HIS MURDERER SHUT THE DOOR, NOT BEAR THE KNIFE MYSELF. BESIDES, THIS DUNCAN HATH BORNE HIS FACULTIES SO MEEK, HATH BEEN SO CLEAR IN HIS GREAT OFFICE, THAT HIS VIRTUES WILL PLEAD LIKE ANGELS

I HAVE NO SPUR TO PRICK THE SIDES OF MY INTENT, BUT ONLY VAULTING AMBITION WHICH O'ER-LEAPS ITSELF AND FALLS ON THE OTHER.

20

BUT SCREW YOUR COURAGE TO THE STICKING PLACE, AND WE'LL NOT FAIL. WHEN DUNCAN IS ASLEEP—WHERETO THE RATHER SHALL HIS DAY'S HARD JOURNEY SOUNDLY INVITE HIM—HIS TWO CHAMBERLAINS WILL I WITH WINE AND WASSAIL SO CONVINCE, THAT MEMORY, THE WARDER OF THE BRAIN, SHALL BE A-FUME, AND THE RECEIPT OF

REASON A LIMBECK ONLY. WHEN IN SWINISH SLEEP THEIR DRENCHĒD NATURES LIES AS IN A DEATH, WHAT CANNOT YOU AND I PERFORM UPON THE UNGUARDED DUNCAN? WHAT NOT PUT UPON HIS SPONGY OFFICERS, WHO SHALL BEAR THE GUILT OF OUR GREAT QUELL?

BRING FORTH MEN-CHILDREN ONLY: FOR THY UNDAUNTED METTLE SHOULD COMPOSE NOTHING BUT MALES.

WILL IT NOT BE RECEIVED, WHEN WE HAVE MARKED WITH BLOOD THOSE SLEEPY TWO OF HIS OWN CHAMBER, AND USED THEIR VERY DAGGERS, THAT THEY HAVE DONE'T?

I AM SETTLED; AND BEND UP EACH CORPORAL AGENT TO THIS TERRIBLE FEAT. AWAY, AND MOCK THE TIME WITH FAIREST SHOW: FALSE FACE MUST HIDE WHAT THE FALSE HEART DOTH KNOW.

WHO DARES RECEIVE IT OTHER, AS WE SHALL MAKE OUR GRIEFS AND CLAMOUR ROAR UPON HIS DEATH?

ACT II SCENE II

THAT WHICH HATH MADE THEM DRUNK HATH MADE ME BOLD; WHAT HATH QUENCHED THEM HATH GIVEN ME FIRE. HARK! PEACE!

IT WAS THE OWL THAT SHRIEKED, THE FATAL BELLMAN, WHICH GIVES THE STERN'ST GOODNIGHT. HE IS ABOUT IT. THE DOORS ARE OPEN, AND THE SURFEITED GROOMS DO MOCK THEIR CHARGE WITH SNORES: I HAVE DRUGGED THEIR POSSETS, THAT DEATH AND NATURE DO CONTEND ABOUT THEM, WHETHER THEY LIVE OR DIE.

WHO'S THERE? WHAT, HO!

ALACK! I AM AFRAID THEY HAVE AWAKED AND 'TIS NOT DONE: THE ATTEMPT AND NOT THE DEED CONFOUNDS US. HARK! I LAID THEIR DAGGERS READY; HE COULD NOT MISS 'EM. HAD HE NOT RESEMBLED MY FATHER AS HE SLEPT, I HAD DONE'T.

MY HUSBAND!

I HAVE DONE THE DEED. DIDST THOU NOT HEAR A NOISE?

I HEARD THE OWL SCREAM AND THE CRICKETS CRY. DID YOU NOT SPEAK?

WHEN?

NOW.

AS I DESCENDED?

AY.

HARK! WHO LIES I' THE SECOND CHAMBER? DONALBAIN.

THIS IS A SORRY SIGHT.

A FOOLISH THOUGHT, TO SAY A SORRY SIGHT.

THERE'S ONE DID LAUGH IN'S SLEEP, AND ONE CRIED 'MURDER!' THAT THEY DID WAKE EACH OTHER. I STOOD AND HEARD THEM. BUT THEY DID SAY THEIR PRAYERS, AND ADDRESSED THEM AGAIN TO SLEEP.

THERE ARE TWO LODGED TOGETHER.

ACT II SCENE III

HERE'S A KNOCKING INDEED! IF A MAN WERE PORTER OF HELL-GATE, HE SHOULD HAVE OLD TURNING THE KEY.

KNOCK, KNOCK, KNOCK! WHO'S THERE, I'THE NAME OF BEELZEBUB? HERE'S A FARMER THAT HANGED HIMSELF ON THE EXPECTATION OF PLENTY. COME IN TIME! HAVE NAPKINS ENOW ABOUT YOU; HERE YOU'LL SWEAT FOR'T.

KNOCK, KNOCK! WHO'S THERE I'THE OTHER DEVIL'S NAME? FAITH, HERE'S AN EQUIVOCATOR, THAT COULD SWEAR IN BOTH THE SCALES AGAINST EITHER SCALE; WHO COMMITTED TREASON ENOUGH FOR GOD'S SAKE, YET COULD NOT EQUIVOCATE TO HEAVEN. O! COME IN, EQUIVOCATOR.

KNOCK, KNOCK, KNOCK! WHO'S THERE? FAITH, HERE'S AN ENGLISH TAILOR COME HITHER FOR STEALING OUT OF A FRENCH HOSE. COME IN, TAILOR; HERE YOU MAY ROAST YOUR GOOSE.

KNOCK, KNOCK; NEVER AT QUIET! WHAT ARE YOU?—BUT THIS PLACE IS TOO COLD FOR HELL. I'LL DEVIL-PORTER IT NO FURTHER.

I HAD THOUGHT TO HAVE LET IN SOME OF ALL PROFESSIONS THAT GO THE PRIMROSE WAY TO THE EVERLASTING BONFIRE.

ANON, ANON! I PRAY YOU, REMEMBER THE PORTER.

29

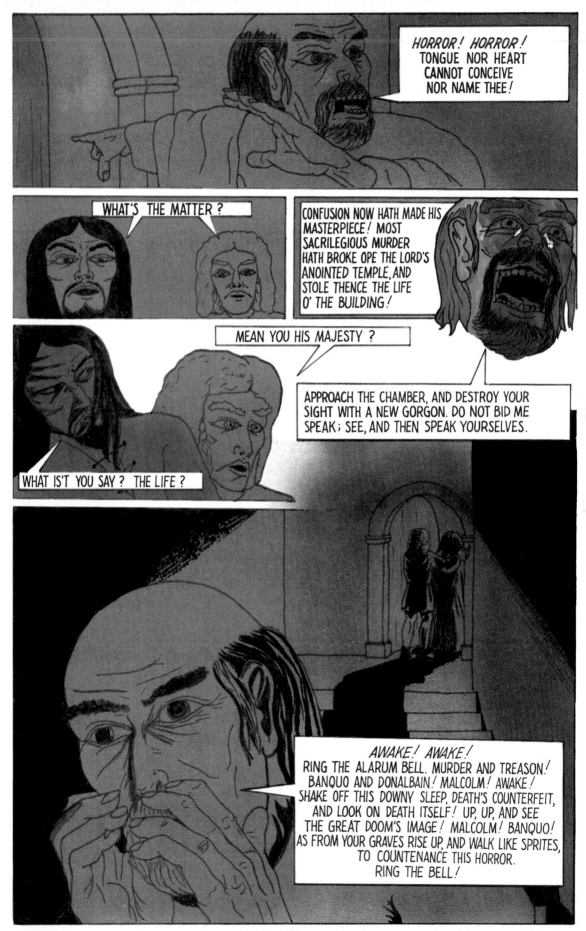

THOSE OF HIS CHAMBER, AS IT SEEMED, HAD DONE'T: THEIR HANDS AND FACES WERE ALL BADGED WITH BLOOD, SO WERE THEIR DAGGERS, WHICH, UNWIPED, WE FOUND UPON THEIR PILLOWS: THEY STARED, AND WERE DISTRACTED; NO MAN'S LIFE WAS TO BE TRUSTED WITH THEM.

O! YET I DO REPENT ME OF MY FURY, THAT I DID KILL THEM.

WHEREFORE DID YOU SO?

WHO CAN BE WISE, AMAZED, TEMPERATE AND FURIOUS, LOYAL AND NEUTRAL, IN A MOMENT? NO MAN. THE EXPEDITION OF MY VIOLENT LOVE OUTRUN THE PAUSER, REASON. HERE LAY DUNCAN, HIS SILVER SKIN LACED WITH HIS GOLDEN BLOOD, AND HIS GASHED STABS LOOKED LIKE A BREACH IN NATURE FOR RUIN'S WASTEFUL ENTRANCE: THERE THE MURDERERS, STEEPED IN THE COLOURS OF THEIR TRADE, THEIR DAGGERS UNMANNERLY BREECHED WITH GORE. WHO COULD REFRAIN, THAT HAD A HEART TO LOVE, AND IN THAT HEART COURAGE TO MAKE'S LOVE KNOWN?

HELP ME HENCE, HO!

LOOK TO THE LADY!

WHY DO WE HOLD OUR TONGUES, THAT MOST MAY CLAIM THIS ARGUMENT FOR OURS?

WHAT SHOULD BE SPOKEN HERE, WHERE OUR FATE, HID IN AN AUGER-HOLE, MAY RUSH AND SEIZE US? LET'S AWAY: OUR TEARS ARE NOT YET BREWED.

NOR OUR STRONG SORROW UPON THE FOOT OF MOTION.

LOOK TO THE LADY.

34

ENTER ROSS AND AN OLD MAN.

THREESCORE AND TEN I CAN REMEMBER WELL;
WITHIN THE VOLUME OF WHICH TIME I HAVE SEEN
HOURS DREADFUL AND THINGS STRANGE, BUT THIS
SORE NIGHT HATH TRIFLED FORMER KNOWINGS.

'TIS UNNATURAL,
EVEN LIKE THE DEED THAT'S DONE. ON TUESDAY LAST
A FALCON, TOWERING IN HER PRIDE OF PLACE,
WAS BY A MOUSING OWL HAWKED AT AND KILLED.

HA , GOOD FATHER,
THOU SEEST THE HEAVENS, AS TROUBLED WITH MAN'S
ACT, THREATENS HIS BLOODY STAGE.
BY THE CLOCK 'TIS DAY, AND YET DARK NIGHT
STRANGLES THE TRAVELLING LAMP:
IS'T NIGHT'S PREDOMINANCE OR THE DAY'S SHAME,
THAT DARKNESS DOES THE FACE OF EARTH ENTOMB,
WHEN LIVING LIGHT SHOULD KISS IT ?

AND DUNCAN'S HORSES – A THING MOST STRANGE AND
CERTAIN – BEAUTEOUS AND SWIFT, THE MINIONS OF
THEIR RACE, TURNED WILD IN NATURE, BROKE THEIR
STALLS, FLUNG OUT, CONTENDING 'GAINST OBEDIENCE,
AS THEY WOULD MAKE WAR WITH MANKIND.

'TIS SAID THEY EAT EACH OTHER.

THEY DID SO,
TO THE AMAZEMENT OF MINE EYES
THAT LOOKED UPON'T.
HERE COMES THE GOOD MACDUFF.
HOW GOES THE WORLD, SIR, NOW ?

WHY, SEE YOU NOT ?

WE HEAR OUR BLOODY COUSINS ARE BESTOWED IN ENGLAND AND IN IRELAND, NOT CONFESSING THEIR CRUEL PARRICIDE, FILLING THEIR HEARERS WITH STRANGE INVENTION. BUT OF THAT TOMORROW, WHEN THEREWITHAL WE SHALL HAVE CAUSE OF STATE CRAVING US JOINTLY. HIE YOU TO HORSE; ADIEU, TILL YOU RETURN AT NIGHT. GOES FLEANCE WITH YOU?

AY, MY GOOD LORD; OUR TIME DOES CALL UPON'S.

I WISH YOUR HORSES SWIFT AND SURE OF FOOT; AND SO I DO COMMEND YOU TO THEIR BACKS. FAREWELL.

LET EVERY MAN BE MASTER OF HIS TIME TILL SEVEN AT NIGHT. TO MAKE SOCIETY THE SWEETER WELCOME, WE WILL KEEP OURSELF TILL SUPPER-TIME ALONE. WHILE THEN, GOD BE WITH YOU!

SIRRAH, A WORD WITH YOU: ATTEND THOSE MEN OUR PLEASURE?

THEY ARE, MY LORD, WITHOUT THE PALACE GATE.

BRING THEM BEFORE US.

TO BE THUS IS NOTHING; BUT TO BE SAFELY THUS.—
OUR FEARS IN BANQUO STICK DEEP,
AND IN HIS ROYALTY OF NATURE REIGNS THAT WHICH
WOULD BE FEARED. 'TIS MUCH HE DARES, AND, TO THAT
DAUNTLESS TEMPER OF HIS MIND, HE HATH A WISDOM
THAT DOTH GUIDE HIS VALOUR TO ACT IN SAFETY.
THERE IS NONE BUT HE WHOSE BEING I DO FEAR;
AND UNDER HIM MY GENIUS IS REBUKED,
AS IT IS SAID MARK ANTONY'S WAS BY CAESAR.
HE CHID THE SISTERS WHEN FIRST THEY
PUT THE NAME OF KING UPON ME,
AND BADE THEM SPEAK TO HIM;
THEN, PROPHET-LIKE, THEY HAILED HIM
FATHER TO A LINE OF KINGS.
UPON MY HEAD THEY PLACED
A FRUITLESS CROWN, AND
PUT A BARREN SCEPTRE
IN MY GRIP,

THENCE TO BE WRENCHED WITH
AN UNLINEAL HAND, NO SON OF
MINE SUCCEEDING. IF IT BE SO,
FOR BANQUO'S ISSUE HAVE I 'FILED
MY MIND: FOR THEM THE GRACIOUS
DUNCAN HAVE I MURDERED;
PUT RANCOURS IN THE VESSEL OF
MY PEACE, ONLY FOR THEM;
AND MINE ETERNAL JEWEL GIVEN
TO THE COMMON ENEMY OF MAN,
TO MAKE THEM KINGS,
THE SEED OF BANQUO KINGS!
RATHER THAN SO, COME FATE INTO
THE LIST AND CHAMPION ME TO
THE UTTERANCE!
WHO'S THERE?

NOW GO TO THE DOOR, AND STAY THERE TILL WE CALL.

WAS IT NOT YESTERDAY WE SPOKE TOGETHER?

IT WAS, SO PLEASE
YOUR HIGHNESS.

BOTH OF YOU KNOW BANQUO WAS YOUR ENEMY.

TRUE, MY LORD.

SO IS HE MINE, AND IN SUCH BLOODY DISTANCE THAT EVERY MINUTE OF HIS BEING THRUSTS AGAINST MY NEAREST OF LIFE: AND THOUGH I COULD WITH BARE-FACED POWER SWEEP HIM FROM MY SIGHT AND BID MY WILL AVOUCH IT, YET I MUST NOT, FOR CERTAIN FRIENDS THAT ARE BOTH HIS AND MINE, WHOSE LOVES I MAY NOT DROP, BUT WAIL HIS FALL WHO I MYSELF STRUCK DOWN: AND THENCE IT IS THAT I TO YOUR ASSISTANCE DO MAKE LOVE, MASKING THE BUSINESS FROM THE COMMON EYE FOR SUNDRY WEIGHTY REASONS.

WE SHALL, MY LORD, PERFORM WHAT YOU COMMAND US.

THOUGH OUR LIVES—

YOUR SPIRITS SHINE THROUGH YOU. WITHIN THIS HOUR AT MOST I WILL ADVISE YOU WHERE TO PLANT YOURSELVES, ACQUAINT YOU WITH THE PERFECT SPY O'THE TIME, THE MOMENT ON'T; FOR'T MUST BE DONE TONIGHT, AND SOMETHING FROM THE PALACE; ALWAYS THOUGHT THAT I REQUIRE A CLEARNESS: AND WITH HIM, TO LEAVE NO RUBS NOR BOTCHES IN THE WORK, FLEANCE HIS SON, THAT KEEPS HIM COMPANY, WHOSE ABSENCE IS NO LESS MATERIAL TO ME THAN IS HIS FATHER'S, MUST EMBRACE THE FATE OF THAT DARK HOUR. RESOLVE YOURSELVES APART; I'LL COME TO YOU ANON.

WE ARE RESOLVED, MY LORD.

I'LL CALL UPON YOU STRAIGHT: ABIDE WITHIN.

IT IS CONCLUDED: BANQUO, THY SOUL'S FLIGHT, IF IT FIND HEAVEN, MUST FIND IT OUT TONIGHT.

ACT III SCENE II

IS BANQUO GONE FROM COURT?

AY, MADAM, BUT RETURNS AGAIN TONIGHT.

SAY TO THE KING I WOULD ATTEND HIS LEISURE FOR A FEW WORDS.

MADAM, I WILL.

NOUGHT'S HAD, ALL'S SPENT, WHERE OUR DESIRE IS GOT WITHOUT CONTENT. 'TIS SAFER TO BE THAT WHICH WE DESTROY THAN BY DESTRUCTION DWELL IN DOUBTFUL JOY.

HOW NOW, MY LORD! WHY DO YOU KEEP ALONE, OF SORRIEST FANCIES YOUR COMPANIONS MAKING, USING THOSE THOUGHTS WHICH SHOULD INDEED HAVE DIED WITH THEM THEY THINK ON? THINGS WITHOUT ALL REMEDY SHOULD BE WITHOUT REGARD: WHAT'S DONE IS DONE.

WE HAVE SCORCHED THE SNAKE, NOT KILLED IT: SHE'LL CLOSE AND BE HERSELF, WHILST OUR POOR MALICE REMAINS IN DANGER OF HER FORMER TOOTH. BUT LET THE FRAME OF THINGS DISJOINT, BOTH THE WORLDS SUFFER, ERE WE WILL EAT OUR MEAL IN FEAR, AND SLEEP IN THE AFFLICTION OF THESE TERRIBLE DREAMS THAT SHAKE US NIGHTLY: BETTER BE WITH THE DEAD, WHOM WE, TO GAIN OUR PEACE, HAVE SENT TO PEACE, THAN ON THE TORTURE OF THE MIND TO LIE IN RESTLESS ECSTASY. DUNCAN IS IN HIS GRAVE; AFTER LIFE'S FITFUL FEVER HE SLEEPS WELL; TREASON HAS DONE HIS WORST: NOR STEEL, NOR POISON, MALICE DOMESTIC, FOREIGN LEVY, NOTHING CAN TOUCH HIM FURTHER.

COME ON; GENTLE MY LORD, SLEEK O'ER YOUR RUGGED LOOKS; BE BRIGHT AND JOVIAL AMONG YOUR GUESTS TONIGHT.

SO SHALL I, LOVE; AND SO, I PRAY, BE YOU. LET YOUR REMEMBRANCE APPLY TO BANQUO;

PRESENT HIM EMINENCE,
BOTH WITH EYE AND TONGUE:
UNSAFE THE WHILE, THAT WE MUST LAVE
OUR HONOURS IN THESE FLATTERING STREAMS,
AND MAKE OUR FACES VIZARDS TO OUR HEARTS,
DISGUISING WHAT THEY ARE.

YOU MUST LEAVE THIS.

O! FULL OF SCORPIONS IS MY MIND, DEAR WIFE;
THOU KNOW'ST THAT BANQUO AND HIS FLEANCE LIVES.

BUT IN THEM NATURE'S COPY'S NOT ETERNE.

THERE'S COMFORT YET; THEY ARE ASSAILABLE.
THEN BE THOU JOCUND. ERE THE BAT HATH FLOWN
HIS CLOISTERED FLIGHT, ERE TO BLACK HECATE'S
SUMMONS THE SHARD-BORNE BEETLE WITH HIS
DROWSY HUMS HATH RUNG NIGHT'S YAWNING PEAL,
THERE SHALL BE DONE A DEED OF DREADFUL NOTE.

WHAT'S TO BE DONE?

BE INNOCENT OF THE KNOWLEDGE, DEAREST CHUCK,
TILL THOU APPLAUD THE DEED. COME, SEELING NIGHT,
SCARF UP THE TENDER EYE OF PITIFUL DAY,
AND WITH THY BLOODY AND INVISIBLE HAND
CANCEL AND TEAR TO PIECES THAT GREAT BOND
WHICH KEEPS ME PALE!
LIGHT THICKENS, AND THE CROW MAKES WING TO
THE ROOKY WOOD: GOOD THINGS OF DAY BEGIN TO
DROOP AND DROWSE, WHILES NIGHT'S BLACK
AGENTS TO THEIR PREYS DO ROUSE.
THOU MARVELL'ST AT MY WORDS: BUT HOLD THEE STILL;
THINGS BAD BEGUN MAKE STRONG THEMSELVES BY ILL.
SO, PRITHEE, GO WITH ME.

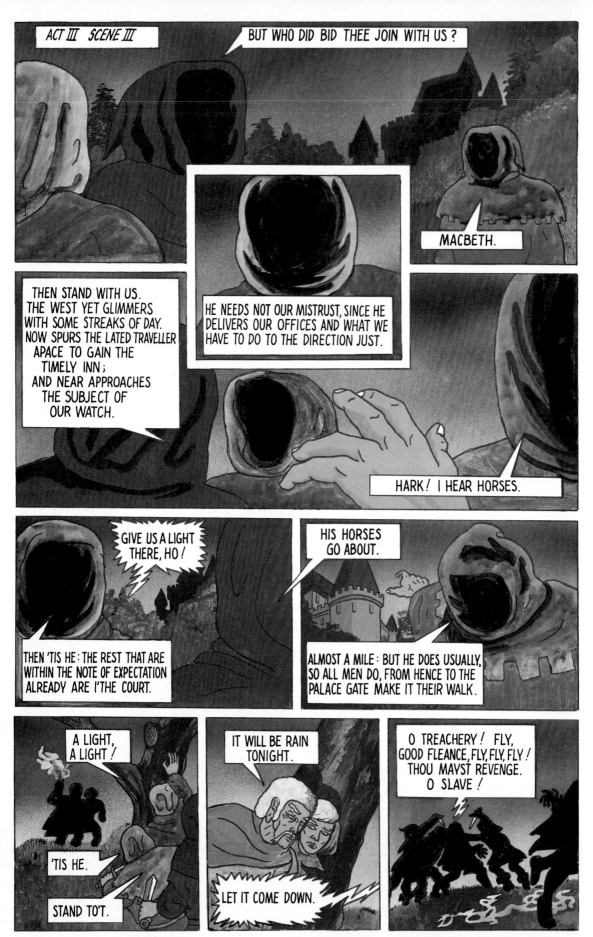

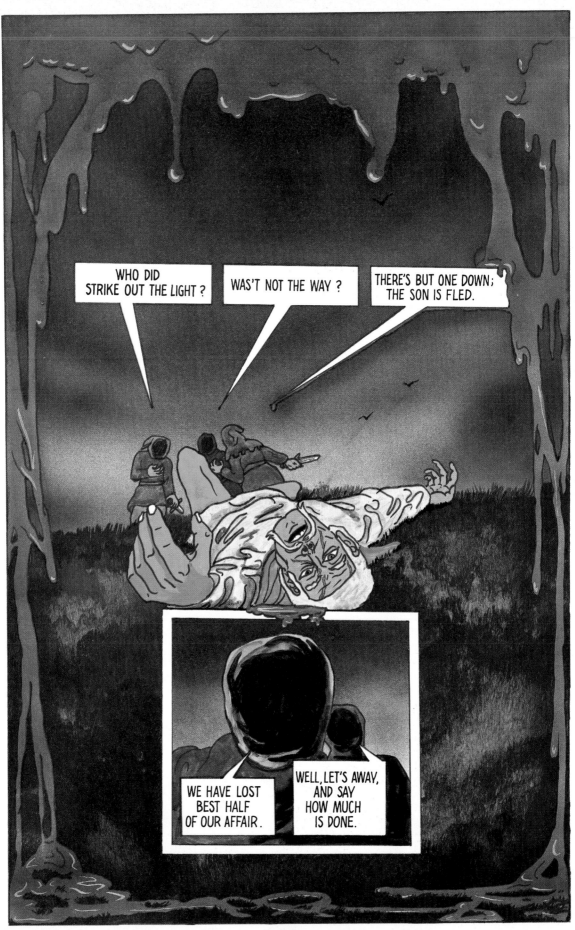

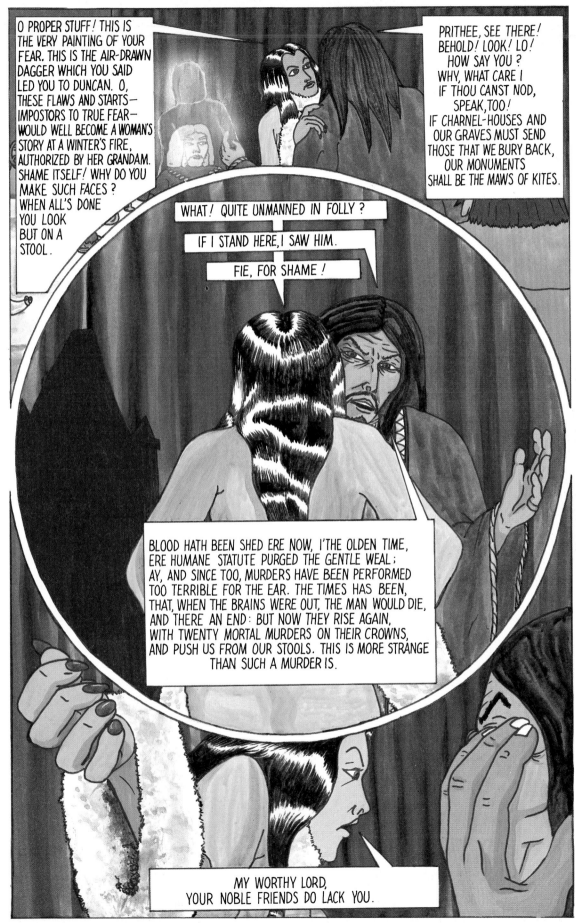

I DO FORGET.
DO NOT MUSE AT ME, MY MOST WORTHY FRIENDS:
I HAVE A STRANGE INFIRMITY, WHICH IS NOTHING
TO THOSE THAT KNOW ME. COME, LOVE AND HEALTH TO ALL;
THEN I'LL SIT DOWN. GIVE ME SOME WINE; FILL FULL!

I DRINK TO THE GENERAL JOY O'THE WHOLE TABLE,
AND TO OUR DEAR FRIEND BANQUO, WHOM WE MISS;
WOULD HE WERE HERE! TO ALL, AND HIM, WE THIRST,
AND ALL TO ALL!

OUR DUTIES, AND THE PLEDGE!

AVAUNT! AND QUIT MY SIGHT! LET THE EARTH HIDE
THEE! THY BONES ARE MARROWLESS, THY BLOOD IS
COLD; THOU HAST NO SPECULATION IN THOSE EYES
WHICH THOU DOST GLARE WITH.

THINK OF THIS, GOOD PEERS,
BUT AS A THING OF CUSTOM: 'TIS NO OTHER;
ONLY IT SPOILS THE PLEASURE OF THE TIME.

WHAT MAN DARE, I DARE.
APPROACH THOU LIKE THE RUGGED RUSSIAN BEAR,
THE ARMED RHINOCEROS, OR THE HYRCAN TIGER;
TAKE ANY SHAPE BUT THAT, AND MY FIRM NERVES
SHALL NEVER TREMBLE. OR BE ALIVE AGAIN,
AND DARE ME TO THE DESERT WITH THY SWORD;
IF TREMBLING I INHABIT THEN, PROTEST ME
THE BABY OF A GIRL. HENCE, HORRIBLE SHADOW!
UNREAL MOCKERY, HENCE!

WHY, SO; BEING GONE, I AM A MAN AGAIN.— PRAY YOU, SIT STILL.

YOU HAVE DISPLACED THE MIRTH, BROKE THE GOOD MEETING, WITH MOST ADMIRED DISORDER.

CAN SUCH THINGS BE, AND OVERCOME US LIKE A SUMMER'S CLOUD, WITHOUT OUR SPECIAL WONDER?

YOU MAKE ME STRANGE EVEN TO THE DISPOSITION THAT I OWE, WHEN NOW I THINK YOU CAN BEHOLD SUCH SIGHTS, AND KEEP THE NATURAL RUBY OF YOUR CHEEKS, WHEN MINE IS BLANCHED WITH FEAR.

WHAT SIGHTS, MY LORD?

I PRAY YOU, SPEAK NOT; HE GROWS WORSE AND WORSE; QUESTION ENRAGES HIM. AT ONCE, GOOD NIGHT. STAND NOT UPON THE ORDER OF YOUR GOING, BUT GO AT ONCE.

GOOD NIGHT; AND BETTER HEALTH ATTEND HIS MAJESTY!

A KIND GOOD NIGHT TO ALL!

IT WILL HAVE BLOOD, THEY SAY; BLOOD WILL HAVE BLOOD. STONES HAVE BEEN KNOWN TO MOVE AND TREES TO SPEAK; AUGURES AND UNDERSTOOD RELATIONS HAVE BY MAGGOT-PIES, AND CHOUGHS, AND ROOKS BROUGHT FORTH THE SECRET'ST MAN OF BLOOD. WHAT IS THE NIGHT?

ALMOST AT ODDS WITH MORNING, WHICH IS WHICH.

HOW SAYST THOU, THAT MACDUFF DENIES HIS PERSON AT OUR GREAT BIDDING?

DID YOU SEND TO HIM, SIR?

I HEAR IT BY THE WAY; BUT I WILL SEND. THERE'S NOT A ONE OF THEM, BUT IN HIS HOUSE I KEEP A SERVANT FEE'D. I WILL TOMORROW— AND BETIMES I WILL— TO THE WEIRD SISTERS: MORE SHALL THEY SPEAK; FOR NOW I AM BENT TO KNOW, BY THE WORST MEANS, THE WORST. FOR MINE OWN GOOD ALL CAUSES SHALL GIVE WAY. I AM IN BLOOD STEPPED IN SO FAR, THAT, SHOULD I WADE NO MORE, RETURNING WERE AS TEDIOUS AS GO O'ER. STRANGE THINGS I HAVE IN HEAD THAT WILL TO HAND, WHICH MUST BE ACTED ERE THEY MAY BE SCANNED.

COME, WE'LL TO SLEEP. MY STRANGE AND SELF-ABUSE IS THE INITIATE FEAR THAT WANTS HARD USE. WE ARE YET BUT YOUNG IN DEED.

YOU LACK THE SEASON OF ALL NATURES, SLEEP.

WHY, HOW NOW, HECATE!
YOU LOOK ANGERLY.

HAVE I NOT REASON, BELDAMS AS YOU ARE,
SAUCY AND OVERBOLD? HOW DID YOU
DARE TO TRADE AND TRAFFIC WITH MACBETH
IN RIDDLES AND AFFAIRS OF DEATH;
AND I, THE MISTRESS OF YOUR CHARMS, THE CLOSE
CONTRIVER OF ALL HARMS, WAS NEVER CALLED TO
BEAR MY PART, OR SHOW THE GLORY OF OUR ART?
AND, WHICH IS WORSE, ALL YOU HAVE DONE HATH BEEN BUT FOR A
WAYWARD SON, SPITEFUL AND WRATHFUL; WHO, AS OTHERS DO,
LOVES FOR HIS OWN ENDS, NOT FOR YOU. BUT MAKE AMENDS
NOW: GET YOU GONE, AND AT THE PIT OF ACHERON
MEET ME IN THE MORNING: THITHER HE WILL COME TO
KNOW HIS DESTINY. YOUR VESSELS AND YOUR SPELLS
PROVIDE, YOUR CHARMS AND EVERYTHING BESIDE.
I AM FOR THE AIR; THIS NIGHT I'LL SPEND UNTO A
DISMAL AND A FATAL END: GREAT BUSINESS MUST
BE WROUGHT ERE NOON: UPON THE CORNER OF
THE MOON THERE HANGS A VAPOROUS DROP
PROFOUND; I'LL CATCH IT ERE IT COME TO GROUND:
AND THAT DISTILLED BY MAGIC SLEIGHTS
SHALL RAISE SUCH ARTIFICIAL SPRITES
AS BY THE STRENGTH OF THEIR
ILLUSION SHALL DRAW HIM ON TO HIS
CONFUSION. HE SHALL SPURN FATE,
SCORN DEATH, AND BEAR HIS
HOPES 'BOVE WISDOM, GRACE,
AND FEAR: AND YOU ALL KNOW
SECURITY
IS MORTALS' CHIEFEST
ENEMY.

HARK!
I AM CALLED;
MY LITTLE SPIRIT, SEE,
SITS IN A FOGGY CLOUD, AND STAYS FOR ME.

COME, LET'S MAKE HASTE; SHE'LL SOON BE BACK AGAIN.

ACT IV SCENE I

THRICE THE BRINDED
CAT HATH MEWED.

THRICE, AND ONCE THE
HEDGE-PIG WHINED.

HARPER CRIES: 'TIS TIME, 'TIS TIME.

ROUND ABOUT THE CAULDRON GO; IN THE POISONED ENTRAILS THROW. TOAD, THAT UNDER COLD STONE DAYS AND NIGHTS HAS THIRTY-ONE. SWELTERED VENOM SLEEPING GOT, BOIL THOU FIRST I'THE CHARMÈD POT.

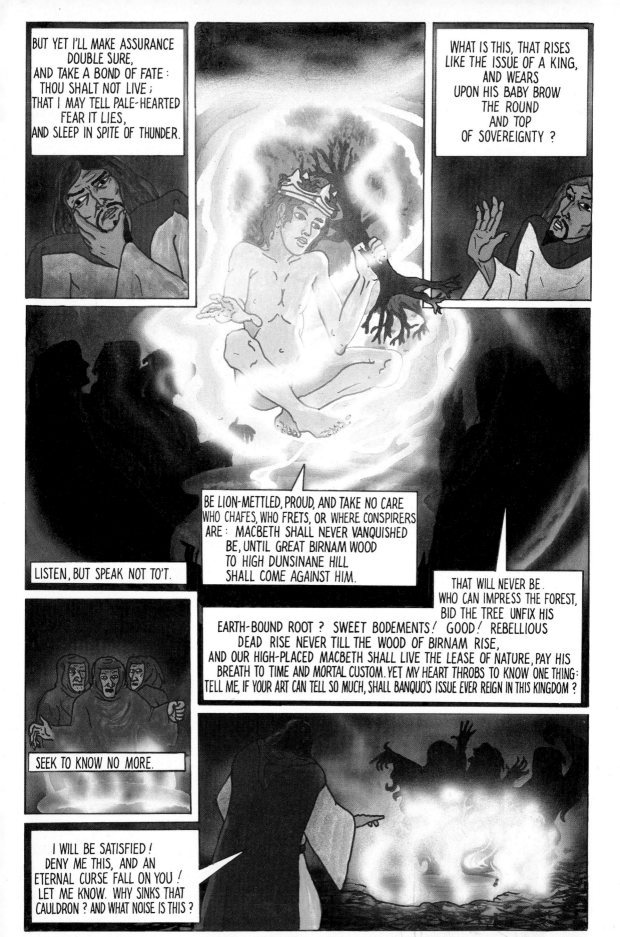

SHOW! SHOW! SHOW!

SHOW HIS EYES, AND GRIEVE HIS HEART; COME LIKE SHADOWS, SO DEPART.

THOU ART TOO LIKE THE SPIRIT OF BANQUO: DOWN!
THY CROWN DOES SEAR MINE EYEBALLS. AND THY HAIR, THOU OTHER GOLD-BOUND BROW, IS LIKE THE FIRST.
A THIRD IS LIKE THE FORMER. FILTHY HAGS! WHY DO YOU SHOW ME THIS? A FOURTH? START, EYES!
WHAT! WILL THE LINE STRETCH OUT TO THE CRACK OF DOOM? ANOTHER YET? A SEVENTH! I'LL SEE NO MORE:
AND YET THE EIGHTH APPEARS, WHO BEARS A GLASS WHICH SHOWS ME MANY MORE; AND SOME I SEE
THAT TWO-FOLD BALLS AND TREBLE SCEPTRES CARRY. HORRIBLE SIGHT! NOW I SEE 'TIS TRUE,
FOR THE BLOOD-BOLTERED BANQUO SMILES UPON ME, AND POINTS AT THEM FOR HIS. WHAT! IS THIS SO?

AY, SIR, ALL THIS IS SO. BUT WHY STANDS MACBETH THUS AMAZĒDLY? COME, SISTERS, CHEER WE UP HIS SPRITES,

AND SHOW THE BEST OF OUR DELIGHTS. I'LL CHARM THE AIR TO GIVE A SOUND,

WHILE YOU PERFORM YOUR ANTIC ROUND, THAT THIS GREAT KING MAY KINDLY SAY OUR DUTIES DID HIS WELCOME PAY.

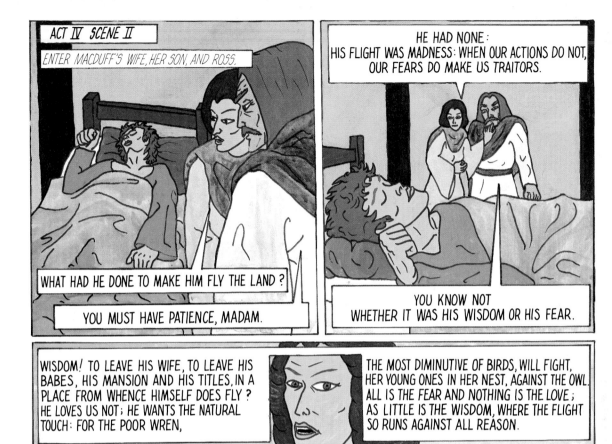

ACT IV SCENE II

ENTER MACDUFF'S WIFE, HER SON, AND ROSS.

WHAT HAD HE DONE TO MAKE HIM FLY THE LAND?

YOU MUST HAVE PATIENCE, MADAM.

HE HAD NONE:
HIS FLIGHT WAS MADNESS: WHEN OUR ACTIONS DO NOT,
OUR FEARS DO MAKE US TRAITORS.

YOU KNOW NOT
WHETHER IT WAS HIS WISDOM OR HIS FEAR.

WISDOM! TO LEAVE HIS WIFE, TO LEAVE HIS BABES, HIS MANSION AND HIS TITLES, IN A PLACE FROM WHENCE HIMSELF DOES FLY? HE LOVES US NOT; HE WANTS THE NATURAL TOUCH: FOR THE POOR WREN,

THE MOST DIMINUTIVE OF BIRDS, WILL FIGHT, HER YOUNG ONES IN HER NEST, AGAINST THE OWL. ALL IS THE FEAR AND NOTHING IS THE LOVE; AS LITTLE IS THE WISDOM, WHERE THE FLIGHT SO RUNS AGAINST ALL REASON.

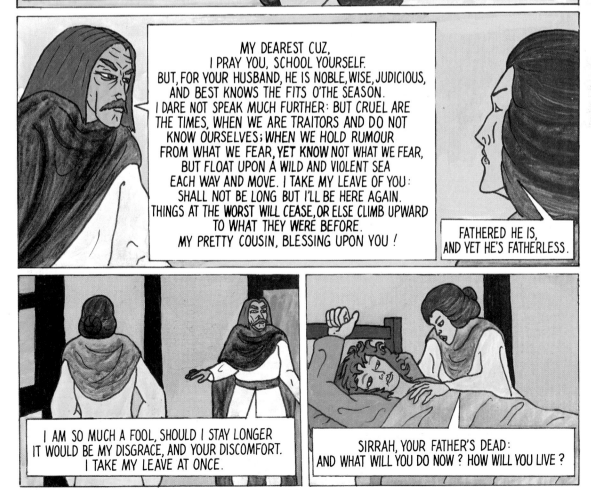

MY DEAREST CUZ,
I PRAY YOU, SCHOOL YOURSELF.
BUT, FOR YOUR HUSBAND, HE IS NOBLE, WISE, JUDICIOUS,
AND BEST KNOWS THE FITS O'THE SEASON.
I DARE NOT SPEAK MUCH FURTHER: BUT CRUEL ARE
THE TIMES, WHEN WE ARE TRAITORS AND DO NOT
KNOW OURSELVES; WHEN WE HOLD RUMOUR
FROM WHAT WE FEAR, YET KNOW NOT WHAT WE FEAR,
BUT FLOAT UPON A WILD AND VIOLENT SEA
EACH WAY AND MOVE. I TAKE MY LEAVE OF YOU:
SHALL NOT BE LONG BUT I'LL BE HERE AGAIN.
THINGS AT THE WORST WILL CEASE, OR ELSE CLIMB UPWARD
TO WHAT THEY WERE BEFORE.
MY PRETTY COUSIN, BLESSING UPON YOU!

FATHERED HE IS,
AND YET HE'S FATHERLESS.

I AM SO MUCH A FOOL, SHOULD I STAY LONGER
IT WOULD BE MY DISGRACE, AND YOUR DISCOMFORT.
I TAKE MY LEAVE AT ONCE.

SIRRAH, YOUR FATHER'S DEAD:
AND WHAT WILL YOU DO NOW? HOW WILL YOU LIVE?

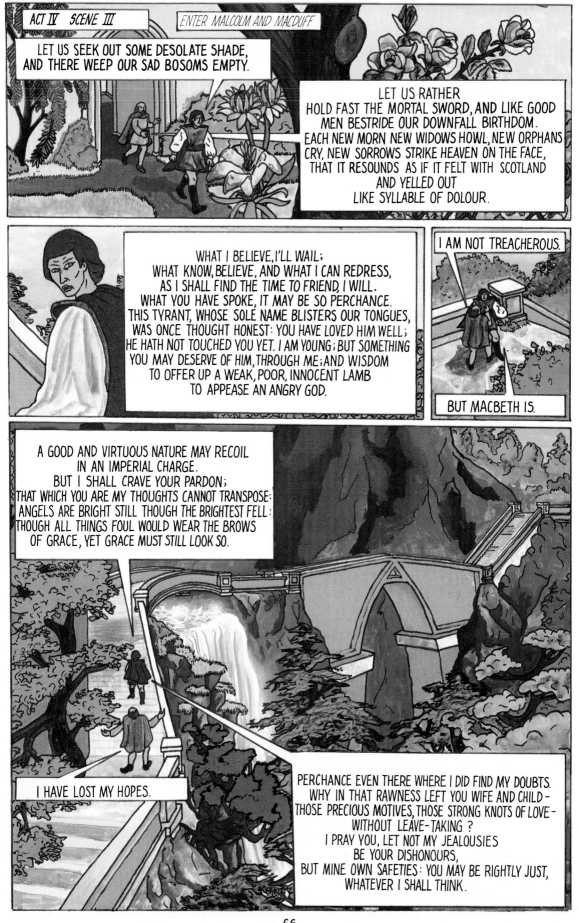

ACT IV SCENE III   ENTER MALCOLM AND MACDUFF

LET US SEEK OUT SOME DESOLATE SHADE,
AND THERE WEEP OUR SAD BOSOMS EMPTY.

LET US RATHER
HOLD FAST THE MORTAL SWORD, AND LIKE GOOD
MEN BESTRIDE OUR DOWNFALL BIRTHDOM.
EACH NEW MORN NEW WIDOWS HOWL, NEW ORPHANS
CRY, NEW SORROWS STRIKE HEAVEN ON THE FACE,
THAT IT RESOUNDS AS IF IT FELT WITH SCOTLAND
AND YELLED OUT
LIKE SYLLABLE OF DOLOUR.

WHAT I BELIEVE, I'LL WAIL;
WHAT KNOW, BELIEVE, AND WHAT I CAN REDRESS,
AS I SHALL FIND THE TIME TO FRIEND, I WILL.
WHAT YOU HAVE SPOKE, IT MAY BE SO PERCHANCE.
THIS TYRANT, WHOSE SOLE NAME BLISTERS OUR TONGUES,
WAS ONCE THOUGHT HONEST: YOU HAVE LOVED HIM WELL;
HE HATH NOT TOUCHED YOU YET. I AM YOUNG; BUT SOMETHING
YOU MAY DESERVE OF HIM, THROUGH ME; AND WISDOM
TO OFFER UP A WEAK, POOR, INNOCENT LAMB
TO APPEASE AN ANGRY GOD.

I AM NOT TREACHEROUS.

BUT MACBETH IS.

A GOOD AND VIRTUOUS NATURE MAY RECOIL
IN AN IMPERIAL CHARGE.
BUT I SHALL CRAVE YOUR PARDON;
THAT WHICH YOU ARE MY THOUGHTS CANNOT TRANSPOSE:
ANGELS ARE BRIGHT STILL THOUGH THE BRIGHTEST FELL:
THOUGH ALL THINGS FOUL WOULD WEAR THE BROWS
OF GRACE, YET GRACE MUST STILL LOOK SO.

I HAVE LOST MY HOPES.

PERCHANCE EVEN THERE WHERE I DID FIND MY DOUBTS.
WHY IN THAT RAWNESS LEFT YOU WIFE AND CHILD -
THOSE PRECIOUS MOTIVES, THOSE STRONG KNOTS OF LOVE -
WITHOUT LEAVE-TAKING ?
I PRAY YOU, LET NOT MY JEALOUSIES
BE YOUR DISHONOURS,
BUT MINE OWN SAFETIES: YOU MAY BE RIGHTLY JUST,
WHATEVER I SHALL THINK.

BLEED, BLEED,
POOR COUNTRY!
GREAT TYRANNY,
LAY THOU THY BASIS SURE,
FOR GOODNESS DARE NOT CHECK THEE:
WEAR THOU THY WRONGS;
THE TITLE IS AFFEERED!
FARE THEE WELL, LORD:
I WOULD NOT BE THE VILLAIN
THAT THOU THINK'ST
FOR THE WHOLE SPACE
THAT'S IN THE TYRANT'S GRASP,
AND IN THE RICH
EAST TO BOOT.

BE NOT OFFENDED:
I SPEAK NOT AS IN ABSOLUTE FEAR OF YOU.
I THINK OUR COUNTRY SINKS BENEATH THE YOKE;
IT WEEPS, IT BLEEDS, AND EACH NEW DAY A GASH
IS ADDED TO HER WOUNDS. I THINK WITHAL,
THERE WOULD BE HANDS UPLIFTED IN MY RIGHT;
AND HERE FROM GRACIOUS ENGLAND HAVE I OFFER
OF GOODLY THOUSANDS. BUT FOR ALL THIS,
WHEN I SHALL TREAD UPON THE TYRANT'S HEAD,
OR WEAR IT UPON MY SWORD, YET MY POOR COUNTRY
SHALL HAVE MORE VICES THAN IT HAD BEFORE,
MORE SUFFER, AND MORE SUNDRY WAYS THAN EVER,
BY HIM THAT SHALL SUCCEED.

WHAT SHOULD HE BE?

IT IS MYSELF I MEAN; IN WHOM I KNOW
ALL THE PARTICULARS OF VICE SO GRAFTED
THAT, WHEN THEY SHALL BE OPENED, BLACK MACBETH
WILL SEEM AS PURE AS SNOW, AND THE POOR STATE
ESTEEM HIM AS A LAMB, BEING COMPARED
WITH MY CONFINELESS HARMS.

NOT IN THE LEGIONS OF HORRID HELL CAN COME
A DEVIL MORE DAMNED IN EVILS TO TOP MACBETH.

I GRANT HIM BLOODY,
LUXURIOUS, AVARICIOUS, FALSE, DECEITFUL,
SUDDEN, MALICIOUS, SMACKING OF EVERY SIN
THAT HAS A NAME: BUT THERE'S NO BOTTOM, NONE,
IN MY VOLUPTUOUSNESS. YOUR WIVES, YOUR DAUGHTERS,
YOUR MATRONS, AND YOUR MAIDS, COULD NOT FILL UP
THE CISTERN OF MY LUST; AND MY DESIRE
ALL CONTINENT IMPEDIMENTS WOULD O'ERBEAR
THAT DID OPPOSE MY WILL. BETTER MACBETH
THAN SUCH A ONE TO REIGN.

BOUNDLESS INTEMPERANCE
IN NATURE IS A TYRANNY; IT HATH BEEN
THE UNTIMELY EMPTYING OF THE HAPPY THRONE,
AND FALL OF MANY KINGS. BUT FEAR NOT YET
TO TAKE UPON YOU WHAT IS YOURS: YOU MAY
CONVEY YOUR PLEASURES IN A SPACIOUS PLENTY,
AND YET SEEM COLD, THE TIME YOU MAY SO HOODWINK.
WE HAVE WILLING DAMES ENOUGH; THERE CANNOT BE
THAT VULTURE IN YOU TO DEVOUR SO MANY
AS WILL TO GREATNESS DEDICATE THEMSELVES,
FINDING IT SO INCLINED.

WITH THIS THERE GROWS
IN MY MOST ILL-COMPOSED AFFECTION SUCH
A STAUNCHLESS AVARICE THAT, WERE I KING,
I SHOULD CUT OFF THE NOBLES FOR THEIR LANDS,
DESIRE HIS JEWELS AND THIS OTHER'S HOUSE;
AND MY MORE-HAVING WOULD BE AS A SAUCE
TO MAKE ME HUNGER MORE, THAT I SHOULD FORGE
QUARRELS UNJUST AGAINST THE GOOD AND LOYAL,
DESTROYING THEM FOR WEALTH.

THIS AVARICE
STICKS DEEPER, GROWS WITH MORE PERNICIOUS ROOT
THAN SUMMER-SEEMING LUST, AND IT HATH BEEN
THE SWORD OF OUR SLAIN KINGS. YET DO NOT FEAR;
SCOTLAND HATH FOISONS TO FILL UP YOUR WILL
OF YOUR MERE OWN. ALL THESE ARE PORTABLE,
WITH OTHER GRACES WEIGHED.

BUT I HAVE NONE.
THE KING-BECOMING GRACES,
AS JUSTICE, VERITY, TEMPERANCE, STABLENESS,
BOUNTY, PERSEVERANCE, MERCY, LOWLINESS,
DEVOTION, PATIENCE, COURAGE, FORTITUDE,
I HAVE NO RELISH OF THEM, BUT ABOUND
IN THE DIVISION OF EACH SEVERAL CRIME,
ACTING IT MANY WAYS. NAY, HAD I POWER, I SHOULD
POUR THE SWEET MILK OF CONCORD INTO HELL,
UPROAR THE UNIVERSAL PEACE, CONFOUND
ALL UNITY ON EARTH.

O SCOTLAND, SCOTLAND!

IF SUCH A ONE BE FIT TO GOVERN, SPEAK:
I AM AS I HAVE SPOKEN.

FIT TO GOVERN!
NO, NOT TO LIVE! O NATION MISERABLE,
WITH AN UNTITLED TYRANT, BLOODY-SCEPTRED,
WHEN SHALT THOU SEE THY WHOLESOME DAYS AGAIN,
SINCE THAT THE TRUEST ISSUE OF THY THRONE
BY HIS OWN INTERDICTION STANDS ACCUSED,
AND DOES BLASPHEME HIS BREED? THY ROYAL FATHER
WAS A MOST SAINTED KING; THE QUEEN THAT BORE THEE,
OFTENER UPON HER KNEES THAN ON HER FEET,
DIED EVERY DAY SHE LIVED. FARE THEE WELL!
THESE EVILS THOU REPEAT'ST UPON THYSELF
HATH BANISHED ME FROM SCOTLAND. O MY BREAST,
THY HOPE ENDS HERE!

MACDUFF, THIS NOBLE PASSION,
CHILD OF INTEGRITY, HATH FROM MY SOUL
WIPED THE BLACK SCRUPLES, RECONCILED MY THOUGHTS
TO THY GOOD TRUTH AND HONOUR. DEVILISH MACBETH
BY MANY OF THESE TRAINS HATH SOUGHT TO WIN ME
INTO HIS POWER, AND MODEST WISDOM PLUCKS ME
FROM OVER-CREDULOUS HASTE: BUT GOD ABOVE
DEAL BETWEEN THEE AND ME! FOR EVEN NOW
I PUT MYSELF TO THY DIRECTION, AND
UNSPEAK MINE OWN DETRACTION, HERE ABJURE
THE TAINTS AND BLAMES I LAID UPON MYSELF,
FOR STRANGERS TO MY NATURE.
I AM YET
UNKNOWN TO WOMAN, NEVER WAS FORSWORN,
SCARCELY HAVE COVETED WHAT WAS MINE OWN,
AT NO TIME BROKE MY FAITH, WOULD NOT BETRAY
THE DEVIL TO HIS FELLOW, AND DELIGHT
NO LESS IN TRUTH THAN LIFE. MY FIRST FALSE SPEAKING
WAS THIS UPON MYSELF. WHAT I AM TRULY
IS THINE AND MY POOR COUNTRY'S TO COMMAND;
WHITHER INDEED, BEFORE THY HERE-APPROACH,
OLD SIWARD WITH TEN THOUSAND WARLIKE MEN,
ALREADY AT A POINT, WAS SETTING FORTH.
NOW WE'LL TOGETHER, AND THE CHANCE OF GOODNESS
BE LIKE OUR WARRANTED QUARREL!
WHY ARE YOU SILENT?

SUCH WELCOME AND UNWELCOME THINGS
AT ONCE, 'TIS HARD TO RECONCILE.

WELL, MORE ANON.—
COMES THE KING FORTH, I PRAY YOU?

AY, SIR. THERE ARE A CREW OF WRETCHED SOULS THAT STAY HIS CURE. THEIR MALADY CONVINCES THE GREAT ASSAY OF ART; BUT, AT HIS TOUCH, SUCH SANCTITY HATH HEAVEN GIVEN HIS HAND, THEY PRESENTLY AMEND.

I THANK YOU, DOCTOR.

WHAT'S THE DISEASE HE MEANS?

'TIS CALLED THE EVIL:
A MOST MIRACULOUS WORK
IN THIS GOOD KING,
WHICH OFTEN, SINCE MY HERE-REMAIN
IN ENGLAND,
I HAVE SEEN HIM DO. HOW HE SOLICITS HEAVEN
HIMSELF BEST KNOWS:
BUT STRANGELY-VISITED PEOPLE,
ALL SWOLLEN AND ULCEROUS, PITIFUL TO THE EYE,
THE MERE DESPAIR OF SURGERY, HE CURES;
HANGING A GOLDEN STAMP ABOUT THEIR NECKS,
PUT ON WITH HOLY PRAYERS; AND 'TIS SPOKEN,
TO THE SUCCEEDING ROYALTY HE LEAVES
THE HEALING BENEDICTION.
WITH THIS STRANGE VIRTUE
HE HATH A HEAVENLY GIFT OF PROPHECY,
AND SUNDRY BLESSINGS HANG ABOUT HIS THRONE
THAT SPEAK HIM FULL OF GRACE.

SEE, WHO COMES HERE?

MY COUNTRYMAN; BUT YET I KNOW HIM NOT.

MY EVER GENTLE COUSIN, WELCOME HITHER.

I KNOW HIM NOW. GOOD GOD, BETIMES REMOVE THE MEANS THAT MAKES US STRANGERS!

SIR, AMEN.

STANDS SCOTLAND WHERE IT DID?

ALAS, POOR COUNTRY, ALMOST AFRAID TO KNOW ITSELF! IT CANNOT BE CALLED OUR MOTHER, BUT OUR GRAVE; WHERE NOTHING, BUT WHO KNOWS NOTHING, IS ONCE SEEN TO SMILE; WHERE SIGHS AND GROANS AND SHRIEKS THAT RENT THE AIR ARE MADE, NOT MARKED; WHERE VIOLENT SORROW SEEMS A MODERN ECSTASY. THE DEAD MAN'S KNELL IS THERE SCARCE ASKED FOR WHO, AND GOOD MEN'S LIVES EXPIRE BEFORE THE FLOWERS IN THEIR CAPS, DYING OR ERE THEY SICKEN.

O, RELATION TOO NICE, AND YET TOO TRUE!

WHAT'S THE NEWEST GRIEF?

THAT OF AN HOUR'S AGE DOTH HISS THE SPEAKER; EACH MINUTE TEEMS A NEW ONE.

HOW DOES MY WIFE?

WHY, WELL.

AND ALL MY CHILDREN?

WELL TOO.

THE TYRANT HAS NOT BATTERED AT THEIR PEACE?

NO, THEY WERE WELL AT PEACE WHEN I DID LEAVE 'EM.

BE NOT A NIGGARD OF YOUR SPEECH: HOW GOES'T?

WHEN I CAME HITHER TO TRANSPORT THE TIDINGS WHICH I HAVE HEAVILY BORNE, THERE RAN A RUMOUR OF MANY WORTHY FELLOWS THAT WERE OUT; WHICH WAS TO MY BELIEF WITNESSED THE RATHER FOR THAT I SAW THE TYRANT'S POWER AFOOT. NOW IS THE TIME OF HELP. YOUR EYE IN SCOTLAND WOULD CREATE SOLDIERS, MAKE OUR WOMEN FIGHT, TO DOFF THEIR DIRE DISTRESSES.

BE'T THEIR COMFORT, WE ARE COMING THITHER. GRACIOUS ENGLAND HATH LENT US GOOD SIWARD AND TEN THOUSAND MEN; AN OLDER AND BETTER SOLDIER NONE THAT CHRISTENDOM GIVES OUT.

HE HAS NO CHILDREN.
ALL MY PRETTY ONES ? DID YOU SAY ALL ?
O HELL-KITE ! ALL ? WHAT, ALL MY PRETTY CHICKENS
AND THEIR DAM AT ONE FELL SWOOP ?

DISPUTE IT LIKE A MAN.

I SHALL DO SO;
BUT I MUST ALSO FEEL IT AS A MAN.
I CANNOT BUT REMEMBER SUCH THINGS WERE,
THAT WERE MOST PRECIOUS TO ME. DID HEAVEN LOOK ON
AND WOULD NOT TAKE THEIR PART ? SINFUL MACDUFF,
THEY WERE ALL STRUCK FOR THEE ! NAUGHT THAT I AM,
NOT FOR THEIR OWN DEMERITS, BUT FOR MINE,
FELL SLAUGHTER ON THEIR SOULS. HEAVEN REST THEM NOW.

BE THIS THE WHETSTONE OF YOUR SWORD: LET GRIEF
CONVERT TO ANGER; BLUNT NOT THE HEART, ENRAGE IT.

O, I COULD PLAY THE WOMAN WITH MINE EYES,
AND BRAGGART WITH MY TONGUE. BUT, GENTLE HEAVENS,
CUT SHORT ALL INTERMISSION; FRONT TO FRONT
BRING THOU THIS FIEND OF SCOTLAND AND MYSELF;
WITHIN MY SWORD'S LENGTH SET HIM;
IF HE 'SCAPE, HEAVEN FORGIVE HIM TOO !

THIS TUNE GOES MANLY.
COME, GO WE TO THE KING; OUR POWER IS READY;
OUR LACK IS NOTHING BUT OUR LEAVE. MACBETH
IS RIPE FOR SHAKING, AND THE POWERS ABOVE
PUT ON THEIR INSTRUMENTS. RECEIVE WHAT CHEER
YOU MAY: THE NIGHT IS LONG THAT NEVER FINDS THE DAY.

ACT V SCENE 1

I HAVE TWO NIGHTS WATCHED WITH YOU, BUT CAN PERCEIVE NO TRUTH IN YOUR REPORT. WHEN WAS IT SHE LAST WALKED?

SINCE HIS MAJESTY WENT INTO THE FIELD, I HAVE SEEN HER RISE FROM HER BED, THROW HER NIGHTGOWN UPON HER, UNLOCK HER CLOSET, TAKE FORTH PAPER, FOLD IT, WRITE UPON'T, READ IT, AFTERWARDS SEAL IT, AND AGAIN RETURN TO BED; YET ALL THIS WHILE IN A MOST FAST SLEEP.

A GREAT PERTURBATION IN NATURE, TO RECEIVE AT ONCE THE BENEFIT OF SLEEP AND DO THE EFFECTS OF WATCHING! IN THIS SLUMBERY AGITATION, BESIDES HER WALKING AND OTHER ACTUAL PERFORMANCES WHAT, AT ANY TIME, HAVE YOU HEARD HER SAY?

THAT, SIR, WHICH I WILL NOT REPORT AFTER HER.

YOU MAY TO ME, AND 'TIS MOST MEET YOU SHOULD.

NEITHER TO YOU NOR ANYONE, HAVING NO WITNESS TO CONFIRM MY SPEECH.

LO YOU! HERE SHE COMES. THIS IS HER VERY GUISE; AND, UPON MY LIFE, FAST ASLEEP. OBSERVE HER; STAND CLOSE.

HOW CAME SHE BY THAT LIGHT?

WHY, IT STOOD BY HER: SHE HAS LIGHT BY HER CONTINUALLY; 'TIS HER COMMAND.

YOU SEE HER EYES ARE OPEN.

AY, BUT THEIR SENSE ARE SHUT.

74

ACT V SCENE II

THE ENGLISH POWER IS NEAR, LED ON BY MALCOLM, HIS UNCLE SIWARD, AND THE GOOD MACDUFF. REVENGES BURN IN THEM; FOR THEIR DEAR CAUSES WOULD TO THE BLEEDING AND THE GRIM ALARM EXCITE THE MORTIFIED MAN.

NEAR BIRNAM WOOD SHALL WE WELL MEET THEM; THAT WAY ARE THEY COMING.

WHO KNOWS IF DONALBAIN BE WITH HIS BROTHER?

FOR CERTAIN, SIR, HE IS NOT. I HAVE A FILE OF ALL THE GENTRY: THERE IS SIWARD'S SON, AND MANY UNROUGH YOUTHS THAT EVEN NOW PROTEST THEIR FIRST OF MANHOOD.

GREAT DUNSINANE HE STRONGLY FORTIFIES. SOME SAY HE'S MAD; OTHERS, THAT LESSER HATE HIM, DO CALL IT VALIANT FURY: BUT, FOR CERTAIN, HE CANNOT BUCKLE HIS DISTEMPERED CAUSE WITHIN THE BELT OF RULE.

WHAT DOES THE TYRANT?

ACT V SCENE III

THE DEVIL DAMN THEE BLACK, THOU CREAM-FACED LOON! WHERE GOT'ST THOU THAT GOOSE LOOK?

BRING ME NO MORE REPORTS; LET THEM FLY ALL!
TILL BIRNAM WOOD REMOVE TO DUNSINANE
I CANNOT TAINT WITH FEAR. WHAT'S THE BOY MALCOLM?
WAS HE NOT BORN OF WOMAN? THE SPIRITS THAT KNOW
ALL MORTAL CONSEQUENCES HAVE PRONOUNCED ME THUS:
'FEAR NOT, MACBETH; NO MAN THAT'S BORN OF WOMAN
SHALL E'ER HAVE POWER UPON THEE.' THEN FLY,
FALSE THANES, AND MINGLE WITH THE ENGLISH EPICURES:
THE MIND I SWAY BY AND THE HEART I BEAR
SHALL NEVER SAG WITH DOUBT NOR SHAKE WITH FEAR.

THERE IS TEN THOUSAND—

GEESE, VILLAIN?

SOLDIERS, SIR.

GO PRICK THY FACE AND OVER-RED THY FEAR,
THOU LILY-LIVERED BOY. WHAT SOLDIERS, PATCH?
DEATH OF THY SOUL! THOSE LINEN CHEEKS OF THINE
ARE COUNSELLORS TO FEAR. WHAT SOLDIERS, WHEY-FACE?

THE ENGLISH FORCE, SO PLEASE YOU.

TAKE THY FACE HENCE.

SEYTON!— I AM SICK AT HEART
WHEN I BEHOLD— SEYTON, I SAY!— THIS PUSH
WILL CHAIR ME EVER OR DIS-SEAT ME NOW.
I HAVE LIVED LONG ENOUGH: MY WAY OF LIFE
IS FALLEN INTO THE SERE, THE YELLOW LEAF;
AND THAT WHICH SHOULD ACCOMPANY OLD AGE,
AS HONOUR, LOVE, OBEDIENCE, TROOPS OF FRIENDS,
I MUST NOT LOOK TO HAVE; BUT IN THEIR STEAD,
CURSES, NOT LOUD, BUT DEEP, MOUTH-HONOUR, BREATH
WHICH THE POOR HEART WOULD FAIN DENY AND DARE NOT.
SEYTON!

WHAT'S YOUR GRACIOUS PLEASURE?

WHAT NEWS MORE?

ALL IS CONFIRMED, MY LORD,
WHICH WAS REPORTED.

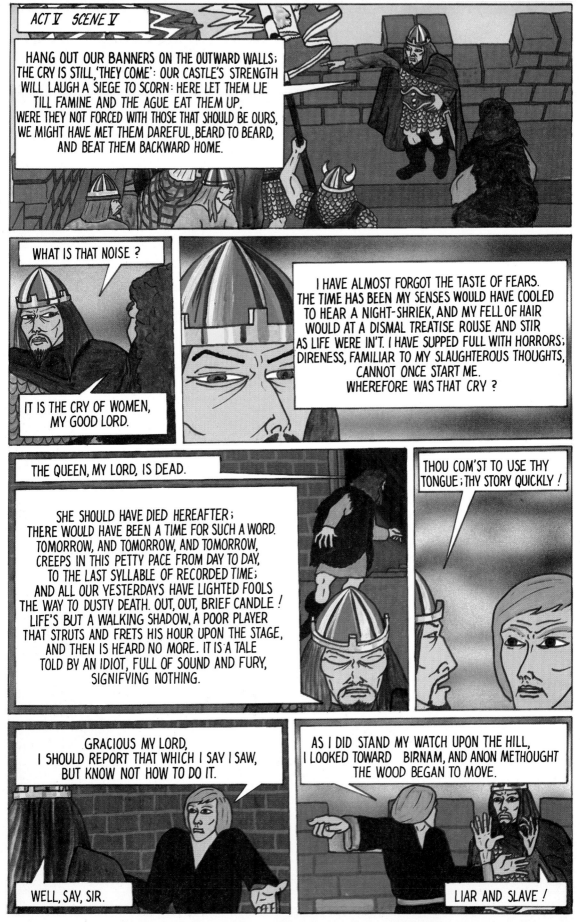

ACT V SCENE V

HANG OUT OUR BANNERS ON THE OUTWARD WALLS;
THE CRY IS STILL, 'THEY COME': OUR CASTLE'S STRENGTH
WILL LAUGH A SIEGE TO SCORN: HERE LET THEM LIE
TILL FAMINE AND THE AGUE EAT THEM UP.
WERE THEY NOT FORCED WITH THOSE THAT SHOULD BE OURS,
WE MIGHT HAVE MET THEM DAREFUL, BEARD TO BEARD,
AND BEAT THEM BACKWARD HOME.

WHAT IS THAT NOISE?

IT IS THE CRY OF WOMEN,
MY GOOD LORD.

I HAVE ALMOST FORGOT THE TASTE OF FEARS.
THE TIME HAS BEEN MY SENSES WOULD HAVE COOLED
TO HEAR A NIGHT-SHRIEK, AND MY FELL OF HAIR
WOULD AT A DISMAL TREATISE ROUSE AND STIR
AS LIFE WERE IN'T. I HAVE SUPPED FULL WITH HORRORS;
DIRENESS, FAMILIAR TO MY SLAUGHTEROUS THOUGHTS,
CANNOT ONCE START ME.
WHEREFORE WAS THAT CRY?

THE QUEEN, MY LORD, IS DEAD.

SHE SHOULD HAVE DIED HEREAFTER;
THERE WOULD HAVE BEEN A TIME FOR SUCH A WORD.
TOMORROW, AND TOMORROW, AND TOMORROW,
CREEPS IN THIS PETTY PACE FROM DAY TO DAY,
TO THE LAST SYLLABLE OF RECORDED TIME;
AND ALL OUR YESTERDAYS HAVE LIGHTED FOOLS
THE WAY TO DUSTY DEATH. OUT, OUT, BRIEF CANDLE!
LIFE'S BUT A WALKING SHADOW, A POOR PLAYER
THAT STRUTS AND FRETS HIS HOUR UPON THE STAGE,
AND THEN IS HEARD NO MORE. IT IS A TALE
TOLD BY AN IDIOT, FULL OF SOUND AND FURY,
SIGNIFYING NOTHING.

THOU COM'ST TO USE THY
TONGUE; THY STORY QUICKLY!

GRACIOUS MY LORD,
I SHOULD REPORT THAT WHICH I SAY I SAW,
BUT KNOW NOT HOW TO DO IT.

WELL, SAY, SIR.

AS I DID STAND MY WATCH UPON THE HILL,
I LOOKED TOWARD BIRNAM, AND ANON METHOUGHT
THE WOOD BEGAN TO MOVE.

LIAR AND SLAVE!

LET ME ENDURE YOUR WRATH IF'T BE NOT SO: WITHIN THIS THREE MILE MAY YOU SEE IT COMING. I SAY, A MOVING GROVE.

IF THOU SPEAK'ST FALSE, UPON THE NEXT TREE SHALL THOU HANG ALIVE, TILL FAMINE CLING THEE.

IF THY SPEECH BE SOOTH,
I CARE NOT IF THOU DOST FOR ME AS MUCH.
I PULL IN RESOLUTION, AND BEGIN TO DOUBT
THE EQUIVOCATION OF THE FIEND THAT LIES LIKE TRUTH:
'FEAR NOT, TILL BIRNAM WOOD DO COME TO DUNSINANE'—
AND NOW A WOOD COMES TOWARD DUNSINANE.
ARM, ARM, AND OUT!
IF THIS WHICH HE AVOUCHES DOES APPEAR,
THERE IS NOR FLYING HENCE, NOR TARRYING HERE.
I 'GIN TO BE AWEARY OF THE SUN,
AND WISH THE ESTATE O'THE WORLD WERE NOW UNDONE.
RING THE ALARUM BELL! BLOW, WIND! COME, WRACK!
AT LEAST WE'LL DIE WITH HARNESS ON OUR BACK.

NOW NEAR ENOUGH: YOUR LEAVY SCREENS THROW DOWN,
AND SHOW LIKE THOSE YOU ARE. YOU, WORTHY UNCLE,
SHALL, WITH MY COUSIN, YOUR RIGHT NOBLE SON,
LEAD OUR FIRST BATTLE. WORTHY MACDUFF AND WE
SHALL TAKE UPON'S WHAT ELSE REMAINS TO DO,
ACCORDING TO OUR ORDER.

FARE YOU WELL.
DO WE BUT FIND THE TYRANT'S POWER TONIGHT,
LET US BE BEATEN IF WE CANNOT FIGHT.

MAKE ALL OUR TRUMPETS SPEAK; GIVE THEM ALL BREATH,
THOSE CLAMOROUS HARBINGERS OF BLOOD AND DEATH.

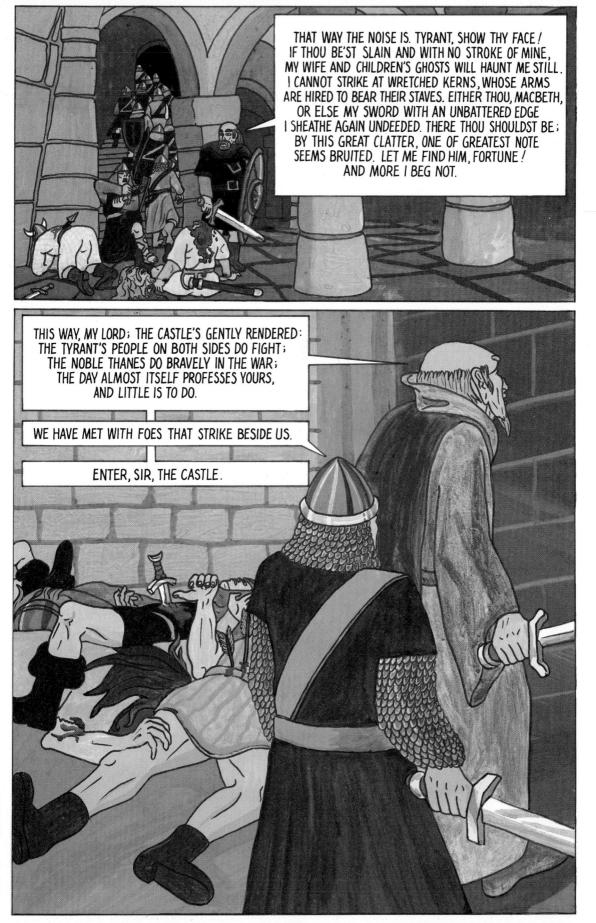

I WILL NOT YIELD
TO KISS THE GROUND BEFORE YOUNG MALCOLM'S FEET,
AND TO BE BAITED WITH THE RABBLE'S CURSE.
THOUGH BIRNAM WOOD BE COME TO DUNSINANE,
AND THOU OPPOSED, BEING OF NO WOMAN BORN,
YET I WILL TRY THE LAST.
BEFORE MY BODY I THROW MY WARLIKE SHIELD.
LAY ON, MACDUFF,
AND DAMNED BE HIM THAT FIRST CRIES,
'HOLD, ENOUGH!'

HAIL, KING! FOR SO THOU ART. BEHOLD, WHERE STANDS
THE USURPER'S CURSÈD HEAD. THE TIME IS FREE.
I SEE THEE COMPASSED WITH THY KINGDOM'S PEARL,
THAT SPEAK MY SALUTATION IN THEIR MINDS,
WHOSE VOICES I DESIRE ALOUD WITH MINE.
HAIL, KING OF SCOTLAND!